A GARLAND
OF STRAW

To my husband José

A Garland of Straw

There is a nomadic people in Africa called the Peuls. When they move from one camping site to another, they leave a garland of straw in a thorn bush, just to say they have been there.

These poems are my garland of straw, my way of saying, "I have been there," in the green places of the earth, yes, and in the deep hidden places where life itself is rooted.

catherine de vinck

a garland
of straw

alleluia press

Funding has been made available by the
NEW JERSEY STATE COUNCIL
ON THE ARTS

ISBN 0-911726-41-1
Library of Congress Catalogue Card No. 81-65684

Published by ALLELUIA PRESS, Box 103, Allendale, N.J. 07401
    and Combermere, Ontario, Canada, KOJ 1LO
PRINTED AND BOUND IN THE UNITED STATES OF AMERICA

CONTENTS

THE PROMISE

"Tell the righteous that it shall be well with them, for they shall eat the fruit of their deeds" (**Is. 3:10**).

This struggle in our flesh
this tug of war
 —red hot cells
  battling pale sluggish death—
it goes on and on
while we are busy elsewhere
  planting and reaping
  gathering our twigs and straws.
It goes on into the night:
even when we find shelter
  in deep caves of sleep
our dreams, visited by hunters
  by stalking beasts, betray us.
By morning we know again
  what it is to be men, women
   keepers of coins, keys and earthen pots;
  to be torn between doubt and belief
  to wonder: are we cherished
   held like marvelous crystals
   to a light we cannot yet reach
  or are we squeezed to the dying
   by some unknown, alien hand?

For the answer
  where shall we look?
Here in the room
  each object gives forth its truth
   like an aura, a scent that endures;
but we change, we grow
  tumble out of the womb
   into a world of high wind
    of battered trees.

And what do we do
and how can we be
    still enough, sure enough
    to taste a fulsome joy
        when the struggle goes on
            murderously within?
Peace: such is the word spoken in the dark
    sown in the night like a glowing seed.
Peace, everywhere
    to people of good will.

I DIE FOR YOU

Cry, and Yahweh will answer; call, and he will say, "I am here!" (Is. 58:9)

Across distances, hear!
More silent than stars
    voices call, not with sound
        with fire. Hear!
They are the thirsty ones
    women frayed like the silk
        of milkweed in autumn
    dried-out men
        with eyes of sand
           lips of sand.
They call:
"We have dipped our hands in bitterness.
See: they are white with salt
    sore from the scraping and the holding.
Wherever we look
    in pots and bowls
    in vases made for flowers
we only see the snowy crystals
    salt, stinking of fish
        the wet essence of our sorrows!"

                ↗   ↗   ↗

"Taken together, they are nothing; their works are nothingness, their images wind and emptiness" (Is. 41:29).

The land is full of soothsayers.
From high places, they shred the language
    into thin strips of words:
fortune, pleasure, happiness
    the right to them
        spoken, written down
        signed and sealed.
The stamping tool
    pressing the melting wax
spells absolute power.

11

We believe, take home, hoard
    all we can:
        days scraped like corn
           from hard husks
        moments we fish out of time
           glittering minnows of joy.
Tomorrow the wind shall buck the door
    break the lock
    pilfer the storage rooms.
What is left?
Where is he who counted?
Where is he who weighed?
Where is he who cut the precious gem
    wove the festive cloth?

🡕   🡕   🡕

*"I am Yahweh, unrivaled, I have not spoken in secret
in some corner of a darkened land. I have not said to
Jacob's descendants, 'Seek me in chaos.' I, Yahweh,
speak with directness, I express myself with clarity"*
(Is. 45:19).

"They come to me wearing masks"
    says the Lord.
"Images of thunder, of plague
    of preying beasts
the masks do not move.
Behind the wooden lids, living eyes;
behind the hinged jaws, living lips
    mouths devouring what they wish
        acres of land, fields and towns
        the portion of the widow
        the pittance of the poor."
"I," says the Lord, "do not hide my face:
    naked is my flesh
        neither black nor white
        neither male nor female
        neither young nor old.
My body is translucent energy
my eyes are gates you can enter.

12

But you, maned and clawed
 like wild animals
 you run through my veins
  hurt me
  tear apart the fine tissue
  of the one great light that I am."
"I bleed over your sunsets"
 says the Lord
"I am in agony in your bedchambers
I scream, nailed to the places
 where you step out of my will
 and spit your lies
  like chunks of rotten fruit."

"Every day, I die for you,"
 says the Lord.

TO SPEAK
NEW WORDS

*"Then one of the seraphim flew to me, holding an
ember which he had taken with tongs from the altar.
He touched my mouth with it"* (Is. 6:6-7).

Beyond the zodiac
where great effigies of light
burn in the night sky
there, behind the black cloth
I saw
      —impossible to see—
angels pulsing with words
      no human throat can sing.
One of them, faster than flight
      flew down to me. He held
      in iron tongs a piece of coal
        red with living fire.
      With this he touched my mouth.
Deprived of speech
      my lips black, sizzling
I reached for the oil jar
      for the water cup.
"Stop!" said the angel.
"Now that your lips are dead
you will speak, not human words
      —these fluttering moths
      hovering on the rim of lamps:
      they are nothing
      they fry in the heat.
Now that your mouth is killed
you will make sounds, speak
      like the wind breathing in emptiness
      like branches breaking
      on frost-cracked days."

WINTER TRAVELING

"Anguish has taken wing, darkness is dispelled for there is no gloom where but now there was distress" (Is. 8:23).

The snaking of roots underground:
    vegetal limbs pushing through the soil.
No gentleness here:
    ruthless power
    working in darkness.
From our bodies
    word-seeds
    children-seeds come forth.
They grow into active life
    bring about new millennia.
We look up
    from our dark places;
our lips open into flowering smiles
our hands wave like branches in the air
    but within
the toil, the struggle go on:
we feed on iron particles
we drink from acrid springs.
What we send into the light
is wrested from the depths
    where we are stretched, pulled
    where we bleed.
Blindly, we move.
Yet, these warm solid shapes
we press through layers of time
rise in the sun
    to shine, to breathe, to last!

TRYING AGAIN

"The people that walked in darkness has seen a great light: on those who live in a land of deep shadow, a light has shone" (Is. 9:1).

Strike a match
hold its flame
    cupped in the hand;
look around
see where you are.
The walls of space are black onyx
    polished to a dark gloss.
A blossom of ice hangs
    from the ceiling: a frozen lamp
      dimmed since millions of years
    slowly swings from invisible cords.
This is a house of sorts
    where we stand chilled
      with nerves taut
      and all impulses retracted like claws.

We are the creatures of this night
    panthers ready to leap
    leopards crouching
      in a landscape of moonlit sands.
We are alone, a multitude
    set alone each to each.
We turn, come full face
    each to each;
eyes meet
    and we downslide in these pools
    to drown alone, each to each.
Bodies are warm, shaped
    with exact knowledge: male and female
    made to be drawn together, fitted
    mouth to mouth and sex to sex.
We hand out our fortune
    waiting for the small change of love
but the coins are flung into the air:

carelessly, they scatter
      rolling out of reach.

We are hungry, walk through winter fields.
The sheaves have been gathered
the grain has been threshed and stored
      in great cylinders of memory.
Can we begin again, haul wet stones
      out of the riverbed
to build a new altar on the ground
      where only rubble stands?
Can we believe again,
      lift the burning match
         the small shivering light?
So little wood is left, fuel enough
      to warm a short-lived moment.
But we shall try again, come together
      each to each
         and say your name
         LORD!

THE STORY-TELLER

"By the strength of my own arm, I have done this, and by my own intelligence, for understanding is mine" (Is. 10:13).

Who shall tell the whole story
   —and for what?
To crack time open
   find the fat worm curled
     its soft mouth moving
      searching for more meat
   —or to gather the years
     into heaps of weapons and bones?
The end is not in sight.

Bent over small fires,
   the women cook:
with huge spoons, they stir the pot
   where centuries boil over
     giving off bitter steam.
The men are elsewhere, busy
   displacing mountains, digging trenches
   making bricks.
They are building
   a place apart from trees, eagles, fish
     from all that tells the story
      since the beginning.
They do not hear
   the voice of the water
     weeping in iron pipes
   the voice of the earth
     crying in pain
      under shovel and drill.
"I am the Story-Teller"
   says the Lord.
"I alone know the whole truth:
at the center of myself
I flower into a three-petaled rose

—no winter here: an infinite blossoming
a shaking of pollen, each grain
exploding into a world
 a new star or a sun.
I speak
 to set my image aswim in your sea
 to be visible flesh and blood.
See how I make my way home
 walking with you
  through your broken gates
  your sagging lives.
Listen: the story is being told
 the most excellent news
 released at last
—breath from my lungs
words from my human voice:
 if you believe in me, you shall not die!"

WHY DO YOU WEEP?

"The light of Israel will become a fire and its Holy One a flame" (Is. 10:17).

Feel the arrangement of your bones
    the structure of your hand
        splayed open
        into five separate fingers.
What they touch:
    small things
    —of metal, cloth or wood—
    smoldering, unknown to you
        in the great electric wave
            the dance of atoms.
See what is carved in the rock
    upland where water falls
    into water, slicing the stone
        with a single liquid thread.
Ancient is your memory:
unknown to you, it travels back
        to the "O" of origin, the moist cave
        the roundness of the womb.

Since the beginning
I speak to you
I am the Word
    of your time
    of your name
    of your tribe and speech.
The figures I trace
    —turning wheels, coils
    of suns and moons—
let them spin and sparkle
    in your blood.
Why do you weep?
Why do you hop on one leg
    pretending you are a crippled bird
        looking for pity?
Hear the marvelous sounds:

20

your heart trembling in its cage
your life shouting life
    through the pores of your skin.
Hear the cadence I tap
    on the drum of your wrist.
You are made to catch the rhythm
    to know you are danced alive
    in the Fire from which no ashes fall:
"I am that Fire"
    says the Lord.

THE MESSAGE WILL
COME THROUGH

> *"There shall be no harm or ruin on all my holy*
> *mountain; for the earth shall be filled with knowl-*
> *edge of the Lord"* (Is. 11:9).

My changeling, how fast you turn
    in the spiral of time!
One moment, you are in the saurian age
    hunting, spear in hand
        some giant aquatic beast.
Next, I see you fully clothed
    tame and unremembering
        by the kitchen door.
A storm is brewing in the east:
    you call in children and cats.

You have forgotten:
    the first garden sank deeper
        than your deepest roots.
Gone, pomegranates
    firewheels of perpetual roses
    freedom without pain!
Yet, in dreams, images return
    rise from dark submerged vaults.
As the wind slashes the lilacs
    beats the windows with an iron fist
something wakes in your mind:
you pace the floor, restless, listening
    to more than rain and wild wind.
The door is closed; there is no crack
    through which to squeeze
        into the landscape of the past:
gone is gone! But the story lives on
    —throbs in your blood—
    of a journey begun long ago
        under a younger moon.
On stormy nights
    in the shaking of the world

you wish to fly out of yourself
　　　into another time, another place:
be still! The message will come through
　　will feed your ancient human heart
　　　　with fresh hope!

THERE IS ONLY
ONE DANCE

*"Sing of Yahweh for he has done marvelous things; let
them be made known to the whole world"* (Is. 12:5).

In that segment of time
in that place
    where I sat silent
    scraped clean of wishes
the voice of the Lord spoke itself
    into my life
    entering from within.
There was a dance
    without steps or music
the form of a dance
    without movement or rhythm.
Unfleshed, I burned
    in the desert-bush thorned with flames
and the voice spelled my name
    in letters white with heat.
Wheels of words revolved
    around a fixed center
printing themselves, circle upon circle
    on the walls of the mind.
The voice housed me
    in a no-where I could see
yet I saw all
    all at once, birth and death
    the beaten iron taking shape
        becoming rod of light
    fields of knowledge bursting open
        scattering seeds of light.

There was a dance:
    light unfolding
    space upon space in which I spun
    further and further
        —my fingertips most distant
        my mouth enormously lost

          my breath no more than faint sigh:
          the trembling of a leaf in a dying wind.

There is only one voice
          and it speaks beyond sound.
There is only one knowing
          and it is beyond craft and wit.
Parchment and scroll crumble to dust;
the bones engraved with the race's history
          winter underground;
overnight, the manna rots
          the quails, unfeathered
vanish in the cooking pots
          which in turn blacken and break.
There is only one dance
          —measure without end—
and here on this earth
the dancer treads on water
          on air
                on fire
and the voice says, "Follow!"

NOT ENOUGH

"The poor are going to feed in my pastures, and beggars rest in safety" (Is. 14:30).

I do not know how to begin:
I am tired, the threads are tangled
    the frame is warped and worn.
I look for a tool
    a needle of sharp knowledge
to piece words together
    into an all-American quilt
      —the pattern, of wheels and rings
       of great eagles spiraling forever
        over corn-yellow fields.

Nothing seems enough!
Why is it that I always wish
    for more than the eye can hold?
The blue wash of the sky
the pleased look in the mirror
    —not enough, not enough!
The spirit hungers, roams
    seeks farther abroad
for something essential to eat:
    muscles and flesh
    and cracking bones of truth.

How could I lie down in winter
    warm in a warm room
the quilt of language pulled over my head
muffling the sound of hurried steps:
    all those people
      cold, starved, looking for food?
Beauty is
    earth
        fire
           water
              and air
    transmuted into bread

26

through long and painful toiling.
Lord, give me the power to be spent
    in the grinding and the shaping
    only of such words
    as will feed the multitude!

IN SILENCE
WE SING

"That day, this song will be sung in the land of Judah"
(Is. 26:1).

The time has come
    to pry open the sealed lids
    to surprise the naked eyes
        with newborn light.
The world glues itself to the retina
colors rush to the brain
    clang and clamor like copper bells.
We had not heard before
    the sound of green
        ringing in tree-towers
    nor the red voice of dawn
        breaking through the night.

The time has come
    to stretch forgotten muscles
    unfold ancient wing-shapes
        hidden in the back of the mind.
Lifting real hands, we rise
    away from the body, yet in the flesh
find pathways through the air
drink the golden liquor of the sun.

O music heard
    —each filament of light
    a string of the lyre
        played by invisible powers
        angels of the morning!
O free, unstudied dance
    leap through circles of fire
        with a speed that is no speed at all
        but intense compressed rhythm
        pulsation of God in the blood!

Beneath us, the beached wrecks:
     a jumble of tools, rusting machines
     bottles, ropes and rags
        the residues of life lived
        in poverty and fear.
No more! Motionless, we glide
     wheeling with the eagle
     calling out, trying to shout
        to name what no letters can spell.
Images break, words crash and shatter
     like clay pots flung upon the rock.
Silence!
     In silence, we sing!

WORLD NEWS

"O Lord, in distress they sought thee, they poured out a prayer when thy chastening was upon them" (Is. 26:16).

We are all standing in the dark
    letter-carriers, messengers
sent across mountain paths
    to deliver the morning news:

      ASIA is drowning
    its thousand hands slipping down
      scraping the hulls of wrecked boats;
    its thousand mouths bitterly rinsed
    its words turning to salt!

We come to speak about an angry woman:
    AFRICA!
Pure black, her body stripped
she rises from her shores
    dripping diamonds and blood.

Muttering like drunken men
we hand out photographs of
    AMERICA:
    sheets printed with replicas
    of people translated into a million dots
      inked on the pages of leaflets and memos.

We are not safe on this planet
this mudball rolling
in a dust of dead stars.
Like pocket-mirrors held to the sun
we burn with many lights
    send signals of ice and fire
      to other spheres.
We ask for entry
    our skins blistered
    our minds breaking out in flames
we stand in the dark by the last door

But love endures:
     poured out, empty
        a wrinkled sack
        a messy bloody rag
the heart goes on beating.
How long?
      Through wars, revolutions
       through the delirium of time
the heart turns like a star
turns upon itself, raying out
      through a thousand wounds
       light more ardent than the sun.

Something moves into the city:
death, as a huge saurian
     with enormous lantern-jaws
slithers through the streets.
People hide in attics and cellars;
the young woman ties a red ribbon
     to the doorknob of her room:
she knows, she has been warned
     it will come around the corner
     clicking its iron teeth
     tearing through mortar and brick.
But a red ribbon
     the love-color of silk
will stop it, will save her
     from the beast.
We shall hook it, cook it
     strip its leather, convert it
     into purse and shoe.
We only need a scarlet ribbon
     one message tied to the barred gate.
The heart will heal
     the wound will be sewed
     with silken thread.
Children of Israel, carry the Book
     in procession through the ages:
your names are hand-written on the pages
     perfumed with terebinth and rosin.

THE RIPE SEASON

Look what happened
    when we were careless
    when we took to the road
        with machine-guns and tanks!

Here are the holy dead
    blue with flies
    lying in summer fields.
Here are their words
    dry pellets, sterile seeds
    flung around for the crows.
Here are the ancestors
    their bones snapped
    the porcelain of their skin
    cracked into spidery patterns.

We are the inheritors:
we cannot pull away
    to navigate by other routes
        with geese and swallows.
We are here to stay:
    feet stuck to the ground
        by gravity, memories, the code
            locked in our blood.
We are muscles oiled with fluid;
we are marvelous hands
    palmed and fingered, touching
    what we can: fur of the cat
        the white edge of the moon
        these acres of body surfaces:
            radiant breasts
            iridescent eyelids
            luminous knee-caps.

We live as usual, we understand
        there is a war going on:
in a panorama of bloody sunsets
        stray bullets are flying
            killing our best thoughts
                murdering our plump, well-feathered dreams.
We shall not be afraid:
we shall continue to work
        to speak, to print ourselves
        on the page of this time, this place.
Our words will come through
        disasters and accidents:
they will bear flowers;
        in the ripe season
they will bear grains and apples.

IN THE DARK
WE DRINK

"Then deep from the earth you shall speak, from low in the dust your words shall come" (Is. 19:4).

We cannot move back:
    the road is blocked
        on which we traveled
        light and easy
        on the track of certitudes.
If we look over our shoulder
we see, at odd angles of time
    women's smiles locked in photographs
    hands held in mid-air
        forever waving goodbyes.
Distantly, voices hail us
    the sound diffused, obstructed
    hardly reaches this present space
    we fill with new words, new shapes.
Yesterday, we could pluck knowledge
    a childish flower
    a blue morning-glory
        planted by the fence
            on the sunny side of the mind.
Now, we crawl through the underground
    our miner's lamp pulsing with heat
        clamped to our forehead.
We choke on black dust;
our eyes grow enormous, strain
    to perceive the golden fleck
        embedded in the face of the rock.
Sometimes we hear water
    dripping from the stone
    icy-cold, speaking
    fresh syllables, almost a song.
We cup our hands:
    in the dark, we drink.

SLIPPING THROUGH

"Yahweh is waiting to be gracious to you, to rise
and take pity on you, for Yahweh is a just God;
happy are all who hope in him" (Is. 30:18).

As we travel, we notice
the map is hastily sketched:
    a filigree of lines
    a vague tracing
—some areas black-streaked
    strata of shadows;
others like empty lots
    gaps bleeding with raw light.

Some days, the sky is flat, dust-colored
    the road, a cold stretch, a slab
        polished by a slick of rain.
We follow it until it runs soft
    into the mud of another year.
In the morning, we enter the forest
    ready for the hunt.
What we chase is a scent
    —we have not seen the fabled beast
    sparks flying from its antlers
    its great head luminous among the trees.
By nightfall, the search is over:
    on our hands, the stench of blood;
    slung over our shoulders
    the dripping pelt.
We do not know
    why we cry these hard heavy tears
    as our body folds upon itself
    creaking on its bony hinges.

There are other places:
    gardens with rings of roses
        rows of incandescent lilies;
    border towns, streets
        crossed over, half-seen

no more than ink stains
flaws on the ancient map.
Finally, a sense comes through
of direction, of peaceful knowing.
The path appears, penciled in sand
raked, brushed, cleared of weed and rubble.
We go forward, rounding out our life
finding, filling our own shape
becoming young, light as children
as we slip through a crack in the rock
into the country of the rising sun.

SAVAGE SONG

*"You shall have a song as in the night when a holy feast
is kept; and gladness of heart, as when one sets out to
the sound of the flute to go to the mountain of the
Lord"* (Is. 30:29).

What beats at the wrist
is not soft tapping
    not drumming of signals
    from an inner world.
It is a savage song, a clamor
    echoing through space
    and louder than sunlight.
We are sealed in this body
    this sound-chamber:
day and night we hear the blood
    circling through arteries and veins;
we hear our raw fleshy heart
    knocking against the walls.
We muffle the sound
    hide it under protective cloth
but the roaring fills our breast
    cannot be stilled.
Among the planets, this one alone
    noisy with such pulsing!
From that deep sightless place
words escape in ritual chants
and what they say breaks through
    the loose mesh of images
to dance free and naked in the wind.

THE DESERT
SHALL REJOICE

*"The wilderness and the dry land shall be glad, the
desert shall rejoice and blossom; like the crocus, it shall
blossom abundantly and rejoice with joy and singing"*
(Is. 35:1-2).

Sand travels:
grain by grain, it moves
        through the cornstalks
moves dry around the wells
        trickling into the gullies
                where the watersnake swims.
The wind, warm with solar heat
blows harsh, speaks
        with a papery tongue.

There is nothing to fear:
the land is wet, soaked
        with thick flowing juices:
                the fluids of many rivers
                the sap of many people.
In the trees of America
        bluebirds eat fleshy berries.
From the rockpiles
from cracks a hairbreadth wide
        lilies rise like oracles
                announcing time without end.
The rains in America clatter
        with kettledrum sounds.
All hollow places silver-fill
        with new water:
                puddles for sparrow beaks
                tranquil bodies of lakes
                overflowing creeks.
They are here to stay, to say:
life is green, no mouth shall thirst
        in America!

Year by year, soundlessly
        the sand travels:
each grain a little wheel turning
        on and on, propelled by moving air.
The wind rolls around, a blowing machine
        lifting the dust on and on
        settling on the roofs
        breaking in the doors
        pouring through the windows
        entering to choke, to kill
        —pure as death: the sand!

                *   *   *

Jesus
        we have no water
            no other food but what grows
            in the desert of the imagination.
How long can we suck on the cactus leaf
        on the bones of a language
            stripped clean of meat?
When we step on the horizon line
        the journey does not end:
it is only a fence of thin trees
        a retaining wall from which to see
            infinitely brilliant
        a world of crystal flakes
            each one a mineral sphere
            a dry sterile fact.
How much farther can we go?
How can we be so still
        and in stillness move at such speed
            across such enormous spaces
        getting nowhere, dressed
        in robes of sand, speaking
        words that fall like sand
            through the funnel of time?

41

There is a name:
    it wakes water-seeds in the ground
    bubbles green at the tip
        of bare branches.
The sound of it
    is of silk ripping open
        letting through cataracts of life.
Our care is to believe
        to draw the name out of our throats
        to kneel at the wet places
            where the Spirit, disguised as water
            bursts through the rock.

THE ALL-KNOWING EYE

"All flesh is grass, and its beauty like the wild flower's: the grass withers, the flowers fade, God remains forever" (Is. 40:7-8).

Look at the women!
    Moon-flowers opening at night
        shaking their scent abroad!
Deep in the heart of their blossoming
    they ache, they weep.
See in the crystal of their tears
    the future stringing itself
        through wet pearls of sorrow.
They sway back and forth
    folding and unfolding gauzy robes.
"We are dancing," they say
but they are caught, rooted
    in earth firmly packed
        around their struggling feet.

Look at the men!
    Sewed and seamed in their sexual skin!
They wake, feel they are
    the dark side of their dreams
    shadows of their glittering twin
        moving elsewhere in pure light.
They are walled in, trapped
    in flesh and stone
—electrons, neutrons, protons
    fizzing about like gnats.
They free-fall through the day
    holding on to their scream
    plummeting down into the evening
        stunned with exhaustion and fear.

It is too late:
    lost is the pattern of the weave
    the working of the threads

fastened to one another
—man to woman, tribe to tribe—
holding together that one fabric
that one splendid earth-cloth!

It is too late: we cannot go
ten thousand years back
to the cave where children suck
the milk of the wilderness
from the breast of a she-wolf.

We have fathered cities
anchored in the rock;
we have searched the outer limits:
our hands, gripping the razor edge
bleed over the cosmos.
We have entered knowledge:
a pleasant room papered
with blueprints and charts.
Behind us—we failed to notice—
doors closed, bolts slipped
into iron locks.
No escape! No release!
No more crossing of the threshold!
The atom is split: death no longer hides
a modest spider balanced in its web:
it hangs in the cloud, a power
ominous and radiant
ready to vaporize the planet.

Forever open
the all-knowing Eye travels
across the ages.
Its sight a needle of light
traces a perfect sphere
a world of time
a world of space.
Under the scanning beam
past, present and future

44

form a single sequence.
The image of yesterday
    older than a millennium of winters
    meshes with today's data
       —traffic by road, by sea
      the air crowded with machines
      the rivers black
        under the falling snow.

"A day is like a thousand years
    and a thousand years like a day,"
    says the Lord.

BE AT REST

"Fear not, for I have redeemed you. I have called you by name, you are mine" (Is. 43:1).

Your body against mine
    says the Lord.
I feel its quivering substance
    its soft shapeless mass
displacing itself, moving away
    a grain at a time
    a year at a time
pulling away from me.
Why are you restless?
You wear your eyes hooded
    like the desert snake;
the words you speak crackle
    dry and hot.
What do you fear?

How astounded you were
    in the beginning
    in the first wet millennium:
you did not know my name
    only the nudge of my will
    stirring your life.

I know the stories you invent
    your betrayals, your lies.
I know your silence
    how silently you approach
    hoping I would not notice
    what you are about to do:
hammer me still, drive the nail
    into the raw nerve of my speech
kill what you cannot tame
    and shape to your wishing.

You cannot escape:
at your right and at your left

before you and beyond
it is I, the Lord, this strange element
in which you are caught
thrashing about
gasping for breath
drowning.
The islands of your hands
remain afloat while you submerge
sink like a stone within my depths.
Stone-flesh
your weight pressed against mine
tears me open.
Be still:
my blood is threading itself
spinning its red filaments
around your limbs.

Child
you cannot move away:
you are the chrysalis in my silk
the slow-waking creature
waiting for the ultimate transport
for wing-power and wind.

Child
your body against mine:
let it rest
not to descend
blind, unfeeling into death
but to rise
conscious of the light
to complete your history
reach your final form.

THIRSTING

*"Should you walk through fire, you will not be scorched
and the flames will not burn you"* (Is. 43:2-3).

Fire is a yellow beast
    eating through the roof of the mind
    screaming
       terror and rage
       terror and rage.
Burning, we run through dark alleys
    our heels winged with flames.
We look for water, hope
    some giant fist will strike the clouds
       release the healing rains.

In the cold heart of winter
a candle glows, a small flame
flickers in the wax. We swarm to it
    little golden moths dancing a moment
       in the heat.
Tomorrow, what will be left in the snow?
    A ring of blackened bodies
    a crispness of dead thoughts?
Will the crow watch?
Will the wolf hear the words
    spilling ashes and blood?

A path opens in the blaze;
the fire-beast cowers, folds its anger
    draws back.
We are led to a place of fountains:
    through curtains of mist
    through silvery vapors
we see hands tenderly lifted
    offering water to our thirst.
One by one by one we are called
    we drink.

SUNBURSTS

*"Behold, I am doing a new thing; how it springs forth,
do you not perceive it?"* (Is. 43:19).

What is it, buzzing in the brain?
    Like a fly caught between screen and glass
something is hurting
    pleading to get out.

We have built a life, a world
    hard and round
        an egg of stone.
We are a city within
    a people besieged, trying
    to break through cold oppressive walls.
We call ourselves men, women
    but what is it beyond the names
        that grimaces and mocks?
Words hold our masks in place:
we could not bear to look
    at naked cheeks, naked lips
    the slopes and caves of the human.
We could get lost, lose ourselves
    in these dark passages
    where the swoosh of blood is racing
    to pump the heart full of rhythm.

It is easier, we think, to dwell
    in abstract empty rooms
    away from what taps and shines
    outside at the window:
        sunbursts, explosions of light
        the perpetual mating-dance
        of air, fire, water and earth.
Dangerous are the new leaves
    waving prayer-flags in the wind.
Will the grass raise its blades
    to slash our flesh, to assault us
        with the miracle of the color green?

Already we begin to hear the lilac buds
        cracking open under our skin.

Whatever it is buzzing in the brain
        —that trapped, hurting spirit—
it will come through its shell of bones
        come dazed into a freedom
        where all things merge as they speak
        their own clear truth.
We shall listen:
        we shall catch the meaning!

THE LONG HOPE

Odd signs on the altar of the street:
    offering of greasy paper
    pips and rinds of wasted lives
    the whole mess trampled, kicked about
        swept by stiff brooms, added
        to some burning heap.
Overhead
    acrid smoke slowly unwinds
    its dark prophecies.
Something must be said
questions must be fished
    wet and glistening from the deep.
We are not looking for coin or ring
    lost talisman, answer to be found
        in the belly of the whale
          as it dies on the beach.
We would like to know
    where we are going
    displaced to what future
    reborn to what fate?

As we go on
    everything moves out, moves away:
in the distance, the years recede
    a retreating army, folding its tents
        rolling up its maps.
The mind—that astronaut free-wheeling
    through open abstract spaces—
    sees the world as a flat print
    where city, stream and mountain
    are smudges equally blurred.

O God
in the street
the cleaning crew rakes up
our yesterdays, pushes to the gutter
our most hopeful words.
We need to know:
can anything be saved?
A scrap of truth
a sliver of beauty
one seedling
for future fields of change?

We shall keep the fire going
in its golden cave;
we shall feed the light
with the pure wax of our care;
we shall watch!
Tomorrow
whatever it is that litters the land
—broken moments, fragments of exploded lives—
will be tenderly gathered
brought back, brought together
for mending, for healing.
Tomorrow
our bodies glistening with oil
wet with the fluids of blessed birth
will come to full waking.
It is enough for today
to be patient
to outwait the winter and the dark.

LOOK AT
THE SUNRISE

"Now I am revealing new things to you, things hidden and unknown to you, created just now, this very moment" (Is. 48:6-7).

The landscape is of painted houses
    of streets where machines roll
—the wheel, that ancient shape
    turns with new speed
        mastering all distances.
Submerged in secrecy, apart from us
    away from the road:
a tree with a guardian crow;
    away from the road
it is the beginning of time
    the moment of creation.

We are asked to fully wake
    to look at the sunrise.
But the language is lost
    that could speak the meaning
    of one black bird clamped
    to the iron rod of a winter tree.

It is not simple to live
    to be sealed in.
Room, mirror, skin
    their limits oppress
yet outside of their frame
lies an alien world:
    objects with cutting edges
    sharp tools, shapes
    other than our own.
So much escapes us
so much moves past and beyond
    this point of time where we stand.
We are often alone, often afraid.

Even our dreams are places of tumult
    of incomprehensible combat.

But our racing blood tells:
    we shall endure another day.
Outside in the snow
    hundreds of wheels speed by.
Overhead, the crow takes to flight
    floats away like a dark cloth.
We must not fear: around us
        faces burn with a lovely human light
            inviting us, begging acceptance.
We draw near, reach out, hear
        all that waits and knocks
            at the door of the future:
                roots in the frozen soil
                fresh shoots of consciousness
                ready to burst into new green words.
We know
        it is the beginning of time
            the moment of creation.

THE SURVIVORS

A sack of beans on a high shelf
        the only food;
tepid water in a rain-barrel
        the only drink;
the planks of the front steps
        rotten through.
We do not know the child
        squatting there
            in the ring of his hunger:
his eyes in the photograph
        forever open, forever recording
        what it is to be small, soft-fleshed
        enclosed in the hard shell
            of a stony land.

We look on, see brown empty fields
        hear the rattle of crumpled leaves
        the papery sound of the wind;
we walk a dusty yellow road
        to the edge of the frame
            edge of the world
and remember we have been there before
        centuries ago.
Words of a foreign tongue
        rise in our throats, words for
            bread   milk
spoken slowly like incantations
        prayers said over a child at nightfall
        to feed the continents of his hunger.

I AM YOUR HOMELAND

"I have branded you on the palms of my hands" (**Is.** 49:16).

See your name, Israel
    burned deep into my hands
    the flesh black, cracked open
    by the firebrand within.
See my body of sand-ripples
    curved here and there into a dry script.
In the waterless land
    my bones lie unassembled:
I thirst, Israel
    give me to drink, cover me
      with a green mantle of rain.

You keep time, watch the years
    notch after notch
    on great wheels of stone.
Day by day, you cast your nets
    bait your traps
but you do not understand my meaning
    what I spoke earlier in the dark:
      a word giving you power
      to invent your life
      beyond heartbeat and breath.
You do not remember: I called you
    pulled you out of the abyss
      over which you dangled, held
      by a thinning thread of faith.
Wearing your flesh, I came to you.
I was nerve and sinew
    a network of muscles and blood;
I was spirit and sex; my thoughts
    rose and fell, moved in drifts
    shuddering under the human weight
    of anguish, incertitude, fear.
Life no longer was flow without end

but a trickle of days
    caught in a small earthen cup.

The story is still being told
    the book still being written.
—I turn the pages, you draw
    whatever you wish: the power was given
    to choose the color, tone, sound
    to illustrate what it is
    to be men, women housed with God
      on a small turning star.
Why, then, are the images bleeding
    like broken mouths?
Why are the words twisted
    like tortured limbs?
Why is the light dimmed
    to a few pulsing dots
    to points of fire pressed
      deep into my palms?

I plucked you from the land
    where you were dying, Israel;
I held you flaming in my hands
    a sharpened brand, a thorn
      of invincible pain.
See these fingers curved around you
    like branches of a great tree
    ready to leaf again, to be roof
    over your head, canopy
    above your altar.
See your name bejeweling my palms
    the letters, ruby-red, flashing
    time and again
    the message of my longing.
I am your homeland, Israel

THE WAY
WILL FIND US

Soon to be released,
    we pace the room
    ears tuned to the sound
        of possible bells
—all the words could get loose
    could ring, saying wild new things.
Crowded together
    hip to hip
we jostle for space.
We have thought about escape
but the cupboards and tables
    are impassable mountains
the chairs, high plateaus
the walls, blue glistening cliffs
    without a foothold.
Water flows from the tap
    pools into oceans:
we float
    on reedy rafts to other shores
    where we find ourselves unchanged
        laboring with the same tools
        dreaming the same world.
Soon we shall be free:
silently turning on oiled hinges
a door will open: the Way will find us.

PASSIONTIDE

*"And the crowds were appalled on seeing him; so dis-
figured did he look that he seemed no longer human;
so will the crowds be astonished at him and kings stand
speechless before him; for they shall see something
never told and witness something never heard before"*
(Is. 53:14-15).

Look
who is coming down the road
    like nothing heard before
    like nothing we can understand:
        that poor shirtless man
        not a cent, not a friend to his name
        dragged by soldiers
        pushed to his death
        by the crowd!
It cannot be
    God cannot be an actual fact
    a statistic, a murdered man
    hanging on crossed posts!

In the past, we lived
    with that figure on a throne
        old Father Time, holding the hourglass
        through which passively we flowed.
From the sun, we took a little fuel;
from the moon, silver words, rhymes
    to rock us to sleep.

Now we must look
    deeper than we know.
Like nothing seen before
    God is a dead Jew
        his body packed with myrrh
        his wounds smeared with oil.
Like nothing we can understand
    he wakes to life
    rises lighter than light
        through dark breaking gates.

The hourglass shatters:
no longer are we jammed together
     pressed down through death's funnel
       like coarse cold sand.
We are free
     move at a changed pace
     and begin anew!

SEND ME WORD

*"The mountains may depart, the hills be shaken, but
my love for you will never leave you"* (Is. 54:10).

Like snowflakes or seeds
all those stars are scattered
    at random it seems
but patterns appear
    —the child in us remembers
    pushing a pencil from dot to dot.
Huge fateful images come in sight
    bear-star, crab, bull and fish
they loom above the earth
    their only portent
      of distances
      of indifferent worlds.
Looking up
    I find their silver cold
      out of scale
      out of tone
    with the colors I wear:
      clay-brown
      the grey of lichened stones
      the mottling of leaf and wood.
I am here
    down here, close to pain
    close to cutting myself
      on the sharp edge of life.
Gone are the plum blossoms
gone even
    the wrinkled pits of their fruit.
The wind moves from the north
    strikes the iron of the sky
    sending out deep winter-sounds.

I need answers
    not star shapes
      hard-glittering
      out of reach;

not these ancient trees
    these monuments of bark and branches
      standing naked in the dark.
I could forage in alleys and corners
    find treasures in garbage heaps:
      the pearl long lost to the swine
      the drachma misplaced for centuries.
But I cannot be soothed
    rocked to sleep
      with fables and magic lights.

Love
    send me word:
I want your name
    branded on my skin
      a great flaming emblem
      to wear under the shirt of pain
        under the grimy coat
        soiled by age and constant handling.
Send me word:
    I wait
      for your coming
      for the kiss of your mouth.

SET US FREE!

"Open up, open up, clear the way, remove all obstacles from the way of my people" (Is. 57:14).

Counting their steps
    children play hopscotch in the street.
Overhead, the sky looks transparent
    made of unsubstantial air
but there is no way out
no spell to cut us loose
    to blow us free like thistle seeds
    across the wind.

Our time is of earth.
We are meshed with one another
    entangled
    like branches of neighboring trees.
And what can we do
    but stretch our arms
    touch, life to life
    give ourselves away?

In the round adobe houses
    of some desert tribes
there is a hole in the roof:
    a central essential place
    for smoke and spirit to journey
    out of confining rooms.
Lord
    through the fire
      over which our days sizzle
    through the cloud
      that stings the eyes
      chokes the lungs
we breathe forth our prayer:
set us free!
We are men, women in ordinary dress
    children jumping over chalk lines
    over continents and centuries:

63

set us free
     to refine our human ways
     to live fully, meshed
          with one another
          with swirling waters
               stars and waves of light.
Lord
     blow us free like thistle seeds
          across the wind!

I AM HERE

"Cry and he will answer, call and he will say, I am here" (Is. 58:9).

All time long, the clamor rises
    not as sound:
    as smoke of a great fire
    stoked with the waste of centuries
        —bloody soil of birth
        stink of animal litter
        stained bandage and dirty shroud.
It all goes to flame,
it all crackles and spits
    red words in the dark.
Cry?
    We cry all time long
    we never cease.
And what appears at our side
    etched in the looking glass?
Pronghorns, a goat's head
    the glowing eyes of the beast.

Oh yes, there are shining moments
    when the day comes in like a good woman
    holding out to us in greeting
        a basket full of eggs and roses.
All things go well:
    we take and eat, we speak
    unwind the layers of meaning
    see the pattern sewn
        with all colors of silks
        —no flaws showing
        no broken threads.
For a moment, neither absence nor grief:
    the hand within reach of another
    the name called, the voice responding.
For a moment, order:
    the room swept
    the broom, the wind at rest.
Whatever it was we felt

65

deep in the gut, the goading pain
of lusting, wanting, raging
eases to a throb hardly perceived.

But one turn of the clock
    and the place is empty
    that yesterday housed
        youth, beauty, strength.
One turn of the mind
    and, by God! there is the ancient weight
        pressing us to the shadows.
We fall, hit the ground
    and the cry rises
        not a sound, a flame
    leaping from our throat.
We could not keep it:
    the time of the child
    the passing through a land
        well watered and greening.
In the looking glass, next to our face
    a hairy filthy mass
    a leering mask, the he-goat
    whispers
        death   desolation   despair!

Call again, scream!
Will God stuff miracles in our mouths
    like rags to muffle our cry?
He will only say, "I am here
    I am with you
        in the whip of the fire
        in the smoky drift
        in the slash of the wound.
All time long
    I am answering
        not with sounding words:
        with power that cancels
            the magic of the beast.
Can you deny the evidence
    —reason beyond reason—
        your quieted heart?"

BREAD TO
THE HUNGRY

"If you do away with the yoke, the clenched fist, the wicked word; if you give your bread to the hungry and relief to the oppressed your light will rise in the darkness and your shadows will become like noon"
(Is. 58:10).

In the grey hour of the evening
    clutching plate and fork
we get ready to eat.
What are these shadows
    clustered by the window?
What is the muffled sound
    outside, by the flame of the gladioli?
Leathery claws grip the windowsill
small shriveled faces peer through the screen.

By the window, at dusk
    the poor of the world assemble.
They are very old
    even the children
    even the little girls
        with eyes like brown moths.
They carry wooden bowls
    of ancient shape;
they do not speak.
Theirs is a country of eternal heat
    of sand lifted like smoke
        by desert winds.

If you give bread to the hungry....

Sugared loaves are stacked
    on shelves and table-tops.
We slice them thickly
    toast them under controlled heat
    set our jaws to the crust.
We are giants sitting on mountain tops
    toying with our food; we eat at leisure

67

chewing great chunks of space
biting a crescent off the moon
—its texture white and soft
made of the finest milled flour.
With strong squared teeth
we grind acres of wheat
cut through the sweet glaze
the honey of the world.
Outside
these ghosts
these silent bony people
stare at us, banging their empty bowls
hard against the walls.

If you give bread to the hungry. . . .

We must hurry:
no time left
soon
no life left in these souring bodies
no light left in our darkening souls.
Come out of the desert
brothers, sisters
sit with us in the open
on the brilliant green grass
and let us share this bread:
the loaves multiplied by love
under caring outstretched hands.

68

ARISE, SHINE

*"Arise, shine; for your light has come, and the glory of
the Lord has risen upon you"* (Is. 60:1).

The present leaks
    drop by time-drop.
"Now," we say
    holding the moment like a flower
    while sap bleeds from the cut stem.
It will not keep
    no matter the care, the gentleness
        of the cradling hand.

We cannot stay where we are:
    the place is windy, set
        on a precarious course.
The pull of gravity anchors our feet
but we spin around, the seasons change
    roses crinkle, turn brown
    and the present drips bad news
        into the future.
What are we doing?
Holding our precious moments
    our little clay lamps moist with oil
we are slow-walking
    along the curve of space
        looking for fire.
Suddenly, at close range
    we hear the sound of flint upon stone;
something flares up, a golden spark
    touches us from within:
we burst into flames
    and life eternal begins.

THE NEW EARTH

"Behold, I create a new heaven and a new earth; and the former things shall not be remembered or come into mind" (Is. 65:17).

Carrying bitter herbs
    we come to the shrine.
There is no altar:
    only a ring of stones;
no sound
    only the wind
        shaking the metallic night.

Can objects ever be the same:
    bedstead, table, chair?
Their solid shape dissolves
    turns vaporous in the dark air.
Can the roof stand, the chimney
    with its puff of grey wool?
The fire shall speak
    as it licks the wall
        with a cat's tongue.
The water shall cool the hand
    soothe the crusted mouth.
And the earth
    —that brown sack full of bones—
shall cushion our sleep.

A new place will be found
    free of nettles and snakes
a soft land of sloping meadows
    where all the bloody linen will be brought
    clean from the laundry rooms
        to bleach and dry under the sun.
Young women will open a path
    through the wild grass
—the delicate line of their bodies
    swollen, ready for birth.

70

THE PRODIGAL

THE PRODIGAL

The clocks have immaculate hands:
    they turn, razor sharp
    slicing time; centuries fall
    in translucent strips
    one upon the other.
What is present, what is past?
Is today's image yesterday's shadow?
Beyond the measure and the count
    a world of pastures:
    wool-puffs in the brambles
    sheep by the salt-licks
    a stream rolling down the gully
        white with speed.

THE INHERITANCE

"There was a man who had two sons: the younger one said to his father, 'Father, give me now my share of the land.'"

A man had two sons.
    One of them
    wears emblems on his heart.
He stands squarely in his morning life
    watching the sun as it rings light
        at the window.
For breakfast, he had
    twenty years of gruel
        milk and mush
    in the same wooden bowl.
Words swarm around him
        —fields   oats   fences—
they quiver in his ears, bees
    without honey, sounds without meaning.
He dreams
    he is eating a long road
    crunching with pebbles;
he sinks his teeth into a town:
    in the town there is an inn
    in the inn, a big brass bed
    between the sheets, a woman.
She is a basket of peaches
she is bread, honeyed and buttered.
"I am hungry," he says
    to his father who is an old man
    printed all over with numbers.
"Life is water, not to be kept in a glass
    but to be spilled, to flow
        past boundaries and remembered hills.
I must find new tools and skills
    assemble an alphabet, learn
        new ways of naming simple things.
A rose is a rose
    until suddenly you see it

74

rising in your mind like an epiphany
like an angel announcing the kingdom."

"Father
    twenty years boil under my skin;
    you own the shirt on my back
    I own the heat under my ribs
        the hidden laughter pressing
        against the chest wall."

"Father
    I can no longer live
    where voices turn
        smooth
    like doors on oiled hinges.
I want cities painted
    orange and lime
    sour to the tongue.
I have walked within your vigilance
    tripping on the rocks you piled
    against my wild wishing.
How can I discover
    goodness is good
    and beauty sweet
unless I leave the shuttered room
    of your will? My thoughts are not oxen
    content to chew the winter straw."

"Father
    to go free I must
    put a match to memory:
    toys and shrines already burn
    with a crisp, definitive sound.
I am already leaving behind
    the summering in Eden, the husked corn
    the fleece of long sleeps.
In the sky of my mind
    someone I do not know
    is holding a quartered apple.

75

I am told a single bite will bring me
    to the center, to the seeds:
    knowledge will be mine
I will eat the world
    I will get drunk on rivers and seas."

THE DEPARTURE

"A few days later, the younger son got together everything he had and left for a distant city where he squandered his money on a life of debauchery."

He sets out in the morning
    drifting like a cloud
    the wind in his back.
No plan: following
    a scent of clover and pine
    a path to a point of intersection
        where the known and the unknown meet
        in dangerous crossing.
Growing new eyes
    the sockets in his face
        fill with hot coals of sight.
"I am on my own," he says
    "bones and flesh
    oiled with freedom."
He moves loosely about
    conscious of passing
        from one form to another
            one world to another.

Shaking off the silence of night-woods
    he travels among voices
        women   children   high-pitched girls
    he listens to words
        how they clickety-clack
        struck like flint
        one against the other
        making fire.
He warms himself
    moves deep within the streets
        within concrete and stone.
He pulls, is pulled
    through the crazy patterns of rooms

through the dry shells of houses
out of the rain, out of the words
that clatter on the roof.

He is a place of presence:
    ears tuned to the incoming waves
    exploring tongue
    eyes peeled open
    in huge petals of sight.
He is feeding on the town:
    traffic dust, elbows on bar-counters
    breasts on window-sills.
"Don't mind me," he says
    as he sets his teeth
    into a small delicate park
    —trees penciled in green
    young girls spread on the grass
    like cream.
Every day the manna falls
    —the little quails with painted beaks
    come winging to his chambers.
There is a singing about that city
    made of a thousand limbs
        a thousand faces
        a thousand hands:
    a singing about life
        one sinuous body rising through
        and coming under
        alive in rubbish and grime
        breathing forth music and smoke.

In the morning, Ishtar came
    goddess of love
        of fruitfulness and war.

"She is a saucer of milk
    constantly tilted and spilling.
I drink, I am the little dog
    on the floor of her life
    lapping her up.

She comes and goes
she flows moon-white
      —her hands pull
      the tides of my blood.
She sells, I buy
      with gold ornaments
         silver weights, ivory and silks.
To please her, I barter what I own:
      ten acres of wheat
      for a jeweled comb.

Am I happy? She is a bird of prey
      an owl soft-feathering my bed;
her beak tears my heart:
      the wound is an eye watching her day by day.
I seek, read the lines of her body
      as prophecies and signs.
Her meaning shifts: at night
      she queens over my dreams.
By sunrise, she sleeps, curled upon herself
      a worm growing fat on the world's meat.
I want to write LOVE
      in the margin of her life
      but the word burns
      a red coal in my palm.
She would not take it.
      I stand between two worlds:
the first, of childhood
      appears framed and fenced;
the second
      lies open, a land
      bleeding with honey and pain.
I am changing, moving outward
      flowing with my woman's milk.
She is a way in the sky, a road-map
      through the stars."

He went out
      cutting through the city
      a swimmer with fast breast-strokes;

he bought more time:
      rain in ropes of pearls
      sun in glittering robes.
When he came back
      the room was empty
      mirrors were dry, deserted pools
      still as stone.
He moved within
      hiking for miles in silver sands.
She came to him, a scorpion of memory
      with stinging tail. Her poison seeped
      in his blood, bringing messages
          pouring acid in his veins.
Around him, the place snapped shut:
      iron screens descended
          curtaining the bed;
      stairs snaked up and down.
          under his feet.
He ran to the streets: the city
      was orange and lime
      hard and sour to the tongue.
"I must go," he says, "where money buys
      mechanical dolls
      big heartless girls, tattooed and tagged.
I will forget her, goddess of the first garden
          apple-round woman
          mother of pleasure and pain."

THE HIRELING

"When he had spent it all, that country experienced a severe famine, and now he began to feel the pinch, so he hired himself out to one of the local inhabitants who put him on his farm to feed the pigs."

There are many doors in his dreams
    intricate locks he cannot break;
    the keys are lost that hung
        from his belt, golden and clanging.
"Open to me," he cries to the moon;
"Open to me," to the rising sun.
No one answers. The window rattles.
Newsprint, the grimace of dead words
      papers the walls.
In the slime of the pig-farm
    his days fall like rotten teeth.
The sow rests on her side
    fat with milk. To her children
    her nipples are rose-buds;
    she grunts with pleasure.
He feeds on berries and mushrooms
    sucks stolen eggs and frogs.
He is weak. "I am turning into water"
    he says to himself, "I am flowing
    into grey nameless fluids.
Is it for me the hawk circles
    for the small pool of my flesh
        the thin juice of my blood?"

At night in the straw, he returns
    to ancient places: a pasture
    quilted with sheep, a courtyard
    where servants stoke a fire
        turn the spit
    —and the stars wheel in the sky
    ages and generations pass
        from light to shadow.

His mind drips with the fat of roasted meat
his thoughts swim in oil
but his hands are empty: he knows
  the cooking pots are dreams
    black and cold over crinkled paper-flames.
What is left to warm his bones?
Who shall carve new eyes, windows
  sharper than diamonds in his soul?
He remembers: in his father's house
  on the kitchen table, a sugar bowl;
  under the lid, the sweet of his life
    white and soft and locked in.

THE FAMINE

"And he would willingly have filled his belly with the husks
the pigs were eating, but no one offered him anything."

Now, in the bitterly north
    he hears the wind bellowing
    in the language of hunger.
"Count my ribs
    coyotes and foxes
tear strips from my chest
    she-demons and ghosts!
I am tired of blackened potatoes
    coffee heated in tin cans
        over the hell-fire of my soul.
—But you don't have me back in your pocket
    Father, not as a handful of jiggling coins
    not yet!
I shall send you postcards
    souvenirs of my travels: Dear Dad,
    see the pig-palace where the great sow
    is enthroned: your son is her servant
        keeper of her brood, cleaner of her bed.
See the master-house set square and stony
see the dogs by the gate
    opening jaws of air. They bark
        soundlessly in my sleep
    tear my days open and bleeding. . . .
Dear Dad, my words roll like grain
    out of a sack, to be scattered
    eaten by crows.
Their husks will be found in bird-droppings
    on the pages of anthologies
    on the plates of students
    in academic halls.
Yes, I have sucked my life dry:
    it lies about like the bone
    of a small finger pointing nowhere.
But I am not ready for a last journey

I can still make a list of what I own:
     right now, my eyes are sending
     tentacles of sight into the twilight
     to touch the little owl, half-hidden
     in the furry darkness of the pine.
My mind can still glide through the maze
     find exits, invent doors, move
        past the teeth of the wolf
          the sting of the asp.
I am not ready to give up
     the half-choked sparrow in my hand
     for a bunch of cockatoos shrieking
        in a distant bush."

It all came so fast, the fever
     shooting through his veins
     boiling in his blood. With veils
     woven with fibers coarser than grass
     death sat smiling at his side.
No instructions were left
     no remedies, no herbs of healing.
His mind no longer wore sweet flesh
     but tunics of repentance, robes
     stained with tears. He heard
     his father calling in the wilderness
        his voice faint, arranging words
        into a map: roads, bridges, paths
        showing the way home.

THE RETURN

"Then he came to his senses and said: 'How many of my father's paid servants have more food than they want, and here I am dying of hunger. I will leave this place and go to my father.'"

So he said, "Yes
    I will pull myself
        through the loops of time past
    return to find the gate
       of my ancestral home.
But I cannot peel the grafted skin
    rip out what the years
       with a surgeon's skill have sewn.
My father cries out to me, his voice
    like a freshet washes me clean.
His love winds the distance, turns
    the wheel, hauls me in."

He crawls through the maze
    knees bleeding on the stone
    one inch at a time
    one millennium at a time
    passing from one ledge to the next
       descending
       ascending
    with the sound
       soft
         of the father's voice. . . .
Overhead, the wingspread of the eagle
    —death in a feather-robe
       with open waiting claws.
But in the greening hedges
    small living eyes of leaves, of birds
    blink in the sun.
This is the time of passage
       time of acceptance
       time of birth.

At night, before him
    a pillar of fire;
by day, a cloud.
He follows.

Fear:
    at eye-level
    the flame of it crackles
    spitting red heat.
It is no simple thing to walk another mile
    to find in the morning's floodlight
        the first road racketing to nowhere.
By noon, the land breaks like glass
    under the hammering sun.
When he was a child, he spoke
    as a child and as a child
    was held and rocked
        in immense aprons of sleep.
Now he is metal in the fire
    a collapsed form
        melting in the endless plain.
He is growing new hands
    a new skin appears under the bubbling blisters.
Can he push himself through
    —muscles and bones and fresh-flowing hope
    wholly new, dressed in tolerance
        and laughter?

The rains march through the land.
They are messengers tattooing the skin.
"Hasten," they say, "hasten
    to bud, to green, to flower;
accept to be broken, to be open
    to bud, to green, to flower."
"Grow," they say, "out of yourself
    to make new roots."
He moves on, coated with slippery fluids
    an infant in the birth-canal
    pressing toward light.

Over the horizon, the father stands:
    master-house, capital-city
    built four-square
        with perfect measure.
His hands are quadrants
his eyes beam highways of light.
The son looks on: he knows
    love is a pillar of fire
    a pyre where all transgressions burn
        anointed with the oil of mercy.

THE ENCOUNTER

"While he was still a long way off, his father saw him and was moved with pity. He ran to the boy, clasped him in his arms and kissed him tenderly."

The kiss
    is most tenderly
    fire poured
        on the straw of his guilt.
The arms around him
    most tenderly
    cradle his withered flesh.
What he wants to do:
    let out a scream
        and run in the sound;
    enter the space, O Father
        where words become the song
    he wants to sing.
Light bounces off earth and sky
    flowing into a baptism:
    he is the fount
    he is the child exposed
      over which light is fitted
        as a rich and golden gown.

"Father, I have sinned against you!
What I desired:
    to go beyond the traced lines
        beyond the iron and the stone
           to a soft world responsive
           to my shaping, to my touch.
What I desired
    was found parceled and without shine.
To seek the warmth of it
    I traveled from place to place
        from story to story
        from woman to woman.

"The Queen of Hearts baked me some tarts
        in her dark oven. I ate for many days
        until she threw me out unsuckled
            screaming for hunger.
In dry summers my many brides
        flowed like water toward my thirst.
I drank:
        cool rivers, sea-bodies
        pulled by moon tides.
The ladies sat on the rocks
        combing their wavy hair, calling
        till I drowned in their streaming.
But no, Father, THIS was not my sin.

"I lived on the rim of nowhere
        in a land of famine and plague.
Year by year, the sand's soft fingers
        reached further, strangling tree-roots
            filling the wells, squeezing life still.
I sat under the sun, asked
        to be cut open by the razor of light;
I sat under the moon and begged
        the ghosted mother to sew me a shroud;
I invited death: it stood by my side
        an armed angel, shining like steel.
I was willing, I wrote a note:
        'Do not save me: I want out!'
But no, Father, THIS was not the sin
        for which I weep most bitter tears.

"Now, Father, I shall confess:
I wanted more than could be found
        —an otherness of sight
        a going everywhere, deep
            into other spaces, other lives;
        a hope:
            no need for lamp
                —being my own light;
            no need for marked path

89

                    —being my own way
Father, I have sinned: I played
          the game of hide-and-seek
          bursting through the wraps
                    of your goodwill
          to own myself, easy and free.
I saw you
          draped in funeral wings
          a crow on a high crag
          waiting to kill
                    the little sparrows of my joys.
I saw you as a wasp with hidden sting
          buzzing in my blood. Father
I did not trust your patient doings:
          this is my sin
                    forgive me!

"Now the boy is dead
          who walked with you by apple-shine
                    under the ripe trees.
A man returns: an image reborn
          in the mirror of your care.
Now perspectives shift:
I see women as they are
          —not willing preys, casualties
          of my lust, of my childish anger
          but daughters of the morning
          calling me with clear voices
                    on the road to daybreak.

"Father, let me serve you:
          in your house and land
let me be one among many.
I do not know what is before me
          but I want my tomorrow cast
                    into the shape of your mercy."

                         90

THE FEAST

"But the father said to his servants: 'Quick, bring out the best robe and put it on him; put a ring on his finger and sandals on his feet. Bring the calf we have been fattening and kill it. We are going to have a feast, a celebration because this son of mine was dead and has come back to life; he was lost and he is found!' And they began to celebrate."

"Father
    the robe I wear trails over the land
        in all shades of purple and gold.
I am home in it, feel its folds
    flowing widely around my life
    making room for my fancies and wonders.
I shall press your signet ring
    deep into the wax of this world
        to seal it with remembrance.
Your love is the current
    in the stream where my life moves
        silver-quick and everlasting.

"Father
    I sit at your table, dip my fingers
    in your dish. My mouth drips
    with meat-juices and wine!
God, I eat—and for the first time
    after so much passing through
    and going under, my hunger lies quiet
        a dog dozing at my feet.

"Father
    all the images return
    with the power to place them
    one next to the other
    in rows of roses and hives and songs!
O Father
    I will go out again
    on the waves of discoveries and dreams
    but not without your counsel
        not without your blessing.

91

The map is wide that will take me
        to travel from this life into another:
but there is time, and I am your son
        the heir to your kingdom!"

92

By the same author (published by ALLELUIA PRESS):

—A TIME TO GATHER, 1968 and 1974
—IKON, 1972 and 1974
—A LITURGY, 1973 and 1977
—A PASSION PLAY, 1975
—A BOOK OF UNCOMMON PRAYERS, 1977 and 1978
—READINGS, 1978
—A BOOK OF EVE (Record), 1979

19   81

One Thousand Copies
Set in Eleven Point Times Roman with Italics
and Eight Point Times Roman with Italics
Printed and Bound by
THEO. GAUS, LIMITED, BROOKLYN, NEW YORK
Constitute the Original Edition